How to Plan Retirement for Women

Guide on Planning Retirement

Carl F. Hendricks

Table of Contents

Introduction

Everyone must deal with the significant life change of retirement, regardless of gender, age, or economic level. Planning for retirement is crucial for women in particular, however, as they have different possibilities and problems in their golden years.

Since women often outlive men, they need more income to support their retirement lifestyle. Throughout their careers, women also often make less money than males, which has an impact on social security, pensions, and savings. In addition, women often take time off work or cut down on their hours to care for their ageing parents, children, or other family members, which further lowers their savings and retirement income.

However, there are many of options for women to enjoy their retirement years as well. Women are free to follow their interests, passions, and hobbies, whether they include volunteering, travelling, education, or launching a new business. In addition, women may improve their well-being and happiness by strengthening their emotional and social bonds with their friends, family, and neighbourhood.

In addition, women may benefit from a range of initiatives and services, including financial education, counselling, and support groups, that can assist them in reaching their retirement objectives.

This book is intended to assist you in retirement planning as a woman and to lead you through the several phases of retirement preparation, including:

- How much money you'll need for retirement and how to begin saving - How to prioritize and create objectives for your retirement
- How to choose the best investments and retirement accounts
- How to budget for medical care and long-term care requirements
- How to revise your legal papers and prepare an estate
- How to get assistance from a professional if you need it

You may design a retirement plan that works for your requirements, choices, and situation by using the procedures and advice in this book. Additionally, you'll be able to overcome obstacles and make use of retirement's chances. Your retirement years will be filled with contentment, stability, and confidence.

Chapter 1

Assess Your Current Situation

You must evaluate your existing financial status before you can begin to prepare for retirement. Understanding where you are, what you have, and what you need to do to reach your retirement objectives will be made easier by doing this.

To evaluate your existing condition, use these three major steps:

1. Determine your cash flow and net value.
2. Calculate your anticipated retirement income and costs.

3. Assess your preparedness for retirement and gap

Determine Your Cash Flow and Net Worth

The gap between your assets and liabilities is your net worth. Your possessions, including your house, vehicle, bank accounts, investments, and retirement funds, are your assets. Your debts, including credit card debt, school loans, auto loans, and mortgages, are your liabilities.

You must make a list of all of your assets and their current valuations, deduct the entire amount of your obligations, and then determine your net worth. Your net worth, or your financial value at a certain moment in time, is the outcome.

The gap between your revenue and spending is what's known as your cash flow. Any money you make, including interest, bonuses, dividends, salary, and rental revenue, is referred to as your income. The money you spend on things like rent, mortgage, utilities, groceries, entertainment, travel, and taxes is known as your costs.

You must keep track of all of your earnings and outlays for a certain time frame, such as a month or a year, to compute your cash flow. Your cash flow, which shows how well you performed financially throughout that time, is the end outcome.

Important markers of your stability and well-being in terms of finances are your cash flow and net worth. They may direct your financial choices and activities and assist you in determining your strengths and shortcomings. You may save and invest more for your retirement, for instance, if your net worth and cash flow are both positive. You must raise your income and decrease your debt and costs if your net worth and cash flow are negative.

Calculate Your Retirement Spending and Income

The money you will get in retirement, including pensions, social security benefits, annuities, and withdrawals from retirement funds, is known as your retirement income.

The money you will spend on housing, health care, travel, and activities during your retirement years is known as your retirement costs.

You must make certain assumptions and estimates based on your present circumstances, your retirement objectives, and your anticipated lifetime to estimate your retirement income and costs. You must also take into account how your income and spending will be impacted by taxes, inflation, and market movements.

A tax counsellor or financial planner may provide you with a more precise and customized estimate.

Assess Your Retirement Preparedness and Shortfall

Your level of preparedness for retirement, as determined by your net worth, cash flow, income, and spending, is known as your retirement readiness. The difference between your retirement income and costs is known as your retirement gap, and it shows you whether or not you have enough savings to meet your demands in retirement.

You must compare your projected retirement income and costs to your retirement objectives and goals to assess your preparation for retirement and the gap that exists. You also need to account for the risks and uncertainties—like inflation, health problems, and market volatility—that might have an impact on your retirement income and spending.

You have a positive retirement gap if your retirement income is higher than or equal to your retirement costs. This indicates that you are either ready to retire or have saved enough money for a comfortable retirement. You have a negative retirement gap if your retirement income is smaller than your retirement costs. This indicates that you either lack the necessary funds for retirement or are not ready to retire.

You may assess your present retirement plan and make any required improvements by taking a look at your retirement preparation and gap. For instance, you may need to work longer, save more, invest more, or cut down on spending if you have a negative retirement gap. You could have more alternatives and flexibility in your retirement planning if your retirement gap is positive.

Chapter 2

Set Your Retirement Vision

Retirement is about more than just your financial situation; it's also about your lifestyle choices. Retirement offers the chance to follow your hobbies, aspirations, and interests to make the most of your golden years and achieve contentment.

But to realize your retirement vision, you must be crystal clear about the kind of retirement you want and the activities you want to engage in with your time and energy. Prioritize the things that are most important to you and strike a balance between your requirements and desires for retirement.

This chapter will walk you through the three processes involved in creating your retirement vision:

1) Specify your retirement goals and way of life.
2) Make a timetable and wish list for retirement.
3) Put your retirement requirements and desires first.

Describe Your Retirement Goals and Way of Living

Your desired manner of living throughout your retirement years is your retirement lifestyle. That covers things like your ideal living situation, your ideal daily schedule, and your ideal pastimes. Your motivation for living a certain lifestyle in retirement is your goal. It covers things like goals, contributions, and learning objectives you have for the years you will be retired.

You should ask yourself some questions to help you identify your retirement lifestyle and goals, such as:

A. Where would you want to reside? Which would you prefer: to travel, downsize, move, or remain in your existing home?

B. How would you want to occupy your time? What are your goals? Do you wish to start a new job, volunteer, work part-time, or pursue a hobby?

C. What kinds of pursuits are you interested in? Are you looking to study, network, work out, or just unwind?

D. What are your hobbies, values, and passions? What brings you joy, contentment, and excitement?

E. What are your hopes, desires, and aspirations? What do you want to accomplish, impart, or discover in your retirement years?

You may define your retirement lifestyle and goals with the use of several tools and techniques, including:

➢ Make a brief and clear declaration about your intended retirement lifestyle and goals, known as a retirement vision statement

➢ Make a vision board for your retirement, a collage of pictures, phrases, and symbols that expresses your ideal retirement way of life and mission

➢ Completing a retirement personality test, a questionnaire designed to evaluate your retirement-related preferences, strengths, and issues

➢ Make a timeline and retirement bucket list.

A retirement bucket list consists of items you'd want to see, do, or go through when you're retired. Anything that you have always wanted to achieve but have never had the chance, money, or time to do might be included. You may spice up your retirement years with excitement, diversity, and enjoyment by creating a retirement bucket list.

Your retirement timeline is a schedule of the things you want to cross off your retirement bucket list, both in terms of when and how. It may assist you with budgeting, planning, and prioritizing your retirement activities. You may also balance your long-term and short-term objectives with the aid of your retirement timetable, and you can modify your plan as your circumstances change.

You must do some actions to compile your retirement wish list and schedule, such as:

1. Come up with ideas for your retirement wish list and put them in writing. To assist you in coming up with ideas, consider using categories like travel, adventure, education, culture, health, family, or community.

2. Examine your retirement wish list and arrange the things in order of significance, practicality, and expense. To rate each item, use a range from 1 to 5, with 1 being the least and 5 being the most.

3. Make a schedule for your retirement and give each item on your retirement bucket list a budget and an aim date. You may make your retirement

timetable with the use of software, a spreadsheet, or a calendar.

4. Regularly review and update your retirement timetable, marking accomplishments as you cross them off. Additionally, you have the option to add new things, edit current items, or remove stuff that you no longer find interesting or relevant.

Set Retirement Needs and Wants in Order of Priority

The things you'll need to acquire or do to sustain your basic level of living and well-being throughout your retirement years are known as your retirement needs. They cover things like food, shelter, healthcare, and taxes. Your retirement wishes are the things you would want to have or do to improve your level of happiness and quality of life when you are retired. They cover things like hobbies, entertainment, travel, and presents.

You must organize your retirement income and resources to meet your retirement objectives and pay your retirement costs to prioritize your requirements and wishes. Along with balancing your immediate and long-term requirements and desires, you also need to modify your saving and spending patterns.

You may prioritize your retirement requirements and goals by using several different techniques and pointers, including:

- Applying the 50/30/20 rule, a budgeting technique that advises allocating 50% of your income to necessities, 30% to desires, and 20% to savings.

- The SMART criteria, a goal-setting technique that calls for making your objectives Specific, Measurable, Achievable, Relevant, and Time-bound, should be used.

- Applying the 4% rule, a withdrawal strategy that advises taking out 4% of your retirement assets in your first year of retirement and increasing the amount yearly to account for inflation

Chapter 3

Build Your Retirement Savings

Increasing your retirement funds is one of the most crucial parts of retirement planning. The money you have saved for retirement throughout your working years is what you will utilize to finance your desired retirement lifestyle.

But saving for retirement is more complicated than just depositing cash into a bank account. Selecting the appropriate retirement funds, allocating your assets and contributions as efficiently as possible, and using employer-sponsored plans and tax advantages are all necessary.

We will walk you through the three processes involved in growing your retirement savings in this chapter:

- ❖ Select the retirement accounts that are ideal for you.

- ❖ Make the most of your donations and asset distribution.

- ❖ Benefit from employer-sponsored programs and tax advantages

- ❖ Select the Retirement Accounts That Are Best for Your Circumstance

Retirement accounts are unique account kinds that provide you with several tax benefits and incentives in addition to enabling you to invest and save money for your future. Retirement accounts can in a variety of forms, including:

1) Individual Retirement Accounts (IRAs), which you may form, maintain, and make contributions to on your own. In 2023, you can contribute up to $6,000 per year (or $7,000 if you are 50 years of age or older). IRAs come in two primary varieties: traditional and Roth.

2) Traditional IRA: You pay taxes on your retirement distributions and may deduct your contributions from your taxable income.

3) Roth IRA: Contributions are tax deductible, but retirement withdrawals are tax-free.

4) 401(k) plans: These are employer-sponsored programs that let you contribute up to $19,500 per year (or $26,000 if you're 50 years of age or older) in 2023. Traditional 401(k) plans and Roth 401(k) plans are the two primary kinds of 401(k) plans.

5) Conventional 401(k): Contributions are tax deductible from your taxable income, and withdrawals are subject to income tax when you're retired.

6) Roth 401(k): Contributions are tax deductible, but retirement withdrawals are tax-free.

7) Alternative retirement account options, include Solo 401(k) plans, SIMPLE IRAs, 403(b) plans, 457 plans, SEP IRAs, and SIMPLE IRAs. These plans are comparable to 401(k) plans but are intended for certain worker groups, like small company owners, teachers, government employees, and independent contractors.

You must take into consideration several aspects to choose the appropriate retirement accounts for your circumstances, including:

I. Your income level and tax bracket, which have an impact on the tax advantages and eligibility for various retirement account kinds.

II. Your anticipated retirement income and tax bracket, which have an impact on your tax obligation and withdrawal plan for various kinds of retirement funds.

III. The amount that your company contributes to your 401(k) plan or other employer-sponsored plan, depending on a portion of your contribution, is known as your employer's matching contribution.

IV. Your retirement accounts' investment options and fees, which refer to the selections and expenses of the funds and securities available for your use.

A financial planner or tax expert should also be consulted for a more precise and tailored proposal.

Make the Most of Your Contributions and Asset Distribution

You must maximize your contributions and asset allocation after deciding which retirement accounts are appropriate for you. The amount of money you deposit into your retirement accounts is known as your contributions, and the distribution of your retirement portfolio across several investment categories, including cash, bonds, and stocks, is known as your asset allocation.

You must adhere to certain rules to maximize your contributions and asset allocation, such as:

1. If applicable, make the most of your contributions or at the least, contribute what it takes to get the full company match. The act of gaining interest on your interest over time is known as compounding, and the more you invest, the more you stand to gain from it.

2. Whenever you get a windfall, bonus, or rise, increase your contributions regularly. You may accelerate the growth of your

retirement funds and meet your retirement objectives sooner if you raise your contributions.

3. Spread your retirement portfolio among a variety of investment kinds with varying degrees of risk and return to diversify your asset allocation. You may lower your exposure to market volatility and improve your long-term performance to a greater extent by diversifying your asset allocation.

4. As your retirement date approaches, switch your retirement portfolio from more aggressive to more cautious investments by adjusting your asset allocation over time. You may better safeguard your retirement funds from market downturns and maintain

your buying power by gradually adjusting your asset allocation.

Benefit from Employer-Sponsored Plans and Tax Reductions

Making use of employer-sponsored programs and tax advantages is another method to increase your retirement savings. Retirement funds provided by your company, such as Solo 401(k) plans, 403(b) plans, 457 plans, SEP IRAs, SIMPLE IRAs, and 401(k) plans, are known as employer-sponsored plans. Tax benefits, which include credits, exemptions, deferrals, deductions, and other tax advantages, are linked to various kinds of retirement plans.

You must use a few tactics and pointers to profit from employer-sponsored plans and tax advantages, including:

A. As soon as you are able, or as soon as you are eligible, enrol in the employer-sponsored plan. Enrolling early allows you to begin investing and saving for retirement as well as to take advantage of any relevant employer match sooner.

B. If at all feasible, make contributions to both a Traditional and a Roth account. When you combine the two kinds of accounts, you may select how and when to take your money depending on your tax status, which can provide you greater flexibility and tax diversification in retirement.

C. If suitable, think about converting to a Roth account. The act of moving funds from a Traditional account to a Roth account and paying taxes on the converted amount is known as a Roth conversion. A Roth conversion may be advantageous if you want to avoid the required minimum distributions (RMDs) that apply to Traditional accounts beyond the age of 72 or if you anticipate being in a higher tax bracket when you retire.

D. If you are qualified, claim the Saver's Credit. If you fulfil certain income and filing status criteria and make contributions to a retirement plan, you may be eligible for the Saver's benefit, a tax benefit. Your tax burden in 2023 may be lowered by up to

$1,000 (or $2,000 if you file jointly) thanks to the Saver's Credit.

Chapter 4

Protect Your Retirement Wealth

It takes more than just increasing your retirement funds to guarantee a safe and enjoyable retirement. Additionally, you must safeguard your retirement assets and income against a variety of dangers and uncertainties that might degrade or deplete them.

The following are a few of the most prevalent and important hazards you might encounter in retirement:

1) Inflation, which lowers the buying power of your money over time by

increasing the average level of prices for goods and services

2) Your longevity, or how long you live, raises the likelihood that you will outlive your retirement assets.

3) Market volatility, which impacts the performance and returns of your retirement portfolio and is defined as the variation in the value of your assets as a result of changes in the financial and economic environment.

We will walk you through the three-step process of safeguarding your retirement assets in this chapter:

Step 1

Control the risks associated with lifespan, inflation, and market volatility.

Step 2

Develop a withdrawal plan and diversify your sources of revenue.

Step 3

Make arrangements for your long-term care, health, and insurance requirements.

Control the Risks of Market Volatility, Longevity, and Inflation

To mitigate the risks associated with inflation, longevity, and market volatility, you need to use certain tactics and methods, like:

1. Invest in securities that are insured against inflation, such as Treasury Inflation-insured Securities (TIPS), which are bonds whose principal and interest payments are adjusted by the rate of inflation.

2. Invest in growth-oriented assets, like equities, which may help you increase your retirement savings since they have the potential to provide long-term returns that are greater than inflation.

3. Invest in dividend-paying stocks, which may provide you with a consistent and increasing income stream that can help you combat inflation. Dividend-paying companies are those that regularly

distribute a percentage of their profits to shareholders.

4. Postpone receiving your social security benefits if you can. Up to the age of 70, your monthly payments will increase the longer you wait to start receiving social security benefits. A further advantage of delaying social security payments is that your yearly cost-of-living adjustments (COLAs), which are determined by the rate of inflation, may go up.

5. Invest in an annuity, which is a contract that offers you a lump sum or a stream of payments in return for a guaranteed income for life or a certain amount of time. You may reduce your chance of outliving your retirement funds and guarantee a steady

flow of income with an annuity. Additionally, if you pick an annuity with an inflation adjustment, your payments will be increased by the rate of inflation.

6. Spread your retirement funds among a variety of investment kinds with varying degrees of risk and return to diversify your retirement portfolio. You may improve your long-term performance and lessen your exposure to market volatility by diversifying your retirement portfolio.

7. To preserve your intended asset allocation and risk tolerance, rebalance or regularly modify your retirement portfolio. You may capture the profits and losses of market changes and prevent overexposure or

underexposure to certain investment types by rebalancing your retirement portfolio.

8. Make use of a dynamic asset allocation, or adjust it over time in response to your evolving requirements, objectives, and situation. You may maximize your risk-return trade-off and adjust to the shifting market circumstances by using a dynamic asset allocation.

Diversify Your Income Sources and Create a Withdrawal Strategy

Developing a withdrawal plan and diversifying your income streams are two more ways to safeguard your retirement assets. The many methods you earn money throughout your retirement years—pension, social security, annuities, dividends, interest, and withdrawals from retirement accounts—are referred to as your income streams. Your withdrawal strategy is a plan that outlines how much, when, and where you take money out of your retirement funds, along with your investment or spending decisions.

You must adhere to certain rules to diversify your sources of income and develop a withdrawal plan, such as:

➢ Have a variety of sources of income or mix several forms of income with varying attributes, such as guaranteed, variable, fixed, or discretionary. Having a variety of income streams may help you manage the risks associated with longevity, inflation, and market volatility in addition to helping you pay for retirement needs.

➢ Earn a combination of tax-free, tax-deferred, and taxable income; alternatively, take withdrawals from various retirement accounts, such as 401(k) plans, Roth IRAs, and Traditional IRAs, which have various tax consequences. You may reduce your tax obligation and maximize your after-tax income by having a combination of taxable, tax-deferred, and tax-free income.

➢ Adhere to the 4% rule, which suggests taking 4% of your retirement savings in your first year of retirement and increasing it by 1% each year to account for inflation. A popular and easy-to-follow withdrawal strategy is the 4% rule, which may help you preserve your level of life and prevent money shortages in retirement. The 4% guideline, however, may not be appropriate for everyone since it relies on several variables, including your asset allocation, spending habits, retirement age, and length of retirement.

➢ Use the bucket technique, which involves dividing your retirement assets into three groups according to your risk tolerance and time horizon. The bucket plan is a more adaptable and dynamic withdrawal technique that may satisfy both your short- and long-term objectives while assisting you in managing market swings. These three pails are:

Bucket 1: Money market funds, certificates of deposit, savings accounts, and other cash equivalents are included in this bucket. Your urgent and necessary costs, such as rent, food, medical bills, and taxes, go into this bucket. This bucket should include enough cash to pay for your living costs for one to two years.

Bucket 2: Annuities, bond funds, and other fixed-income instruments are included in this bucket. This is the designated area for your intermediate and optional costs, which include presents, entertainment, travel, and hobbies. This bucket should include enough cash to pay for your living needs for three to ten years.

Bucket 3: Growth-oriented assets, such as stocks, stock funds, and real estate, are included in this bucket. This bucket is for your ambitious, long-term costs, including schooling, charitable giving, and leaving a legacy. This bucket should include enough cash to support your living expenditures for ten or more years.

Make a plan for your long-term care, insurance, and medical needs.

Making plans for your long-term care, health care, and insurance requirements is the last step to safeguarding your retirement assets. Your healthcare requirements are any medical services and treatments, such as doctor visits, prescription drugs, surgeries, and hospital stays, that you could need throughout your retirement years. The personal and custodial services you may need if you can no longer do some of the fundamental activities of daily living, such as eating, dressing, bathing, and moving, are known as long-term care requirements.

Your insurance requirements include those policies and products that may help you pay for long-term care and medical expenses, as well as safeguard your retirement assets against unforeseen circumstances like sickness, accidents, litigation, and natural disasters.

You must take some actions to prepare for your insurance, long-term care, and medical requirements. These include:

1. Compute your expected medical and long-term care expenditures or the out-of-pocket spending you could have for medical and long-term care requirements in your retirement years. Your predicted longevity, your family history, your lifestyle choices, your present health, and the rate of inflation are just a few of the variables you might use to estimate your expenditures.

2. Sign up for Medicare, the government health insurance program for those 65 years of age or older and those with

certain medical conditions or impairments. Medicare is divided into four sections: Part D (prescription medication coverage), Part C (Medicare Advantage), Part B (medical insurance), and Part A (hospital insurance). During your first enrollment period, which lasts for seven months and starts three months before your 65th birthday and ends three months after your birthday, you may apply for Medicare.

3. Take into account supplementary insurance, which is extra coverage you may get to offset Medicare's gaps and restrictions (including deductibles, copayments, coinsurance, and out-of-pocket maximums).

Supplemental insurance comes in two primary flavours: Medicare Advantage and Medigap.

4. Medigap: Medigap is a kind of private insurance that supplements Part A and Part B of Original Medicare by paying for some of the expenses that Part B does not.

5. Medicare Advantage: Medicare Advantage is a kind of private insurance that provides an extra benefit, such as wellness programs, vision, dental, and hearing care, in addition to your regular Medicare benefits.

6. Invest in long-term care insurance, a kind of private insurance that pays for all or part of the expenses associated with long-term care services, including adult day care, assisted living, home health care, and nursing homes. In addition to providing you with more alternatives and control over your long-term care options, long-term care insurance may help you protect your retirement assets. Long-term care insurance may be acquired at any age, but if you obtain it while you are younger and in better condition, the rates will be cheaper.

Make sure your other insurance plans, which include life, disability, homes, vehicle, and umbrella insurance, are current and sufficient for your retirement requirements by reviewing them. Depending on your retirement objectives, income, costs, and assets, you may need to modify your coverage, premiums, deductibles, and beneficiaries.

Chapter 5

Enjoy Your Retirement Life

Keeping up with retirement is a process that involves both financial and emotional aspects. Retirement is an opportunity to reflect on your principles, pursue your hobbies, and enjoy your accomplishments. Retirement also offers opportunities to overcome obstacles like ageing, loneliness, and redefining oneself.

We will walk you through the three stages necessary to enjoy your retirement life in this chapter:

A. Adapt to the social and emotional changes that come with retirement

B. Follow your interests and passions after retirement.

C. Reinvest in your community and create a lasting impression.

Adapt to Retirement's Emotional and Social Changes

Retirement may alter your life on numerous social and emotional levels, including:

1) Losing your identity and position at work, might have an impact on your confidence, feeling of purpose, and self-worth

2) Possessing more free time and flexibility, which might mean

rearranging your schedule, your life's structure, and its balance.

3) Modifying how you interact, communicate, and assist with your family, friends, and coworkers.

4) Experiencing novel experiences and emotions, such as relief, excitement, pleasure, boredom, worry, melancholy, or regret

You must use a few methods and tactics to help you cope with the emotional and social shifts that come with retirement, including:

A. Rethink who you are, or find and accept your new self and position in retirement, outside of your job and profession. To do this, consider your beliefs, interests, and talents. You may also make a personal mission statement that encapsulates your vision and objectives for your retirement years.

B. Based on your requirements, preferences, and priorities, plan and arrange your daily, weekly, and monthly retirement activities and duties. This is known as a retirement schedule. You may do this by creating your retirement timetable with the use of software, a planner, or a calendar.

C. Keep up and grow your social network, or connect and engage with current relatives, friends, and coworkers; in retirement, form new relationships and friendships. You may do this by joining different communities and groups like clubs, courses, or volunteer organizations, as well as by utilizing a variety of platforms and channels including social media, email, phone, and online forums.

D. Control your emotions and sentiments, or recognize, embrace, and find a healthy, constructive method to deal with them when you're retired. This may be accomplished via a variety of techniques and tools, including writing, meditation, therapy, and support groups.

Pursue Your Passions and Hobbies in Retirement

Retirement offers the chance to follow your interests and pastimes, or the activities, knowledge, or experiences that you find enjoyable, gratifying, and satisfying. In addition to improving your physical, mental, and emotional well-being, pursuing your interests and hobbies in retirement may give your retirement years significance and purpose.

Following your interests and passions in retirement might provide the following advantages:

- ❖ Increasing your level of health and fitness by partaking in physical activities like walking, bicycling, swimming, or gardening that may increase your strength, vitality, and immunity.

❖ Playing games, puzzles, reading, writing, or other mental exercises that test your cognitive abilities may help to stimulate your brain and memory.

❖ Expanding your artistic expression and creativity via creative pursuits like painting, music, photography, or crafting that allow you to use your imagination and skills.

❖ Growing your knowledge and abilities by participating in educational pursuits that stimulate your interest and learning, such as attending seminars, enrolling in classes, or learning a language.

❖ Investigating your passions and aspirations via daring pursuits that extend your viewpoints and vistas, like travelling, camping, or jumping

In order to follow your interests and passions after retirement, you must do the following:

1. Determine your interests and passions, or make a list of the things you like doing, learning, or experiencing because they make you happy, fulfilled, and satisfied. To assist you in coming up with ideas, you

might utilize categories like adventure, education, creativity, brain, and health.

2. Set priorities for your interests and pastimes, or order the things you like doing, learning, or experiencing in terms of significance, viability, and expense. To rate each item, use a range from 1 to 5, with 1 being the least and 5 being the most.

3. Follow your interests and passions; alternatively, begin and keep doing, learning, or experiencing the things that you find fulfilling, joyful, and satisfying. To assist you in pursuing your interests and passions, you may utilize a variety of tools and resources,

including books, periodicals, websites, apps, and podcasts.

4. Connect and engage with others who share your interests and passions so they may encourage, inspire, and support you. - Share your passions and hobbies. To help you communicate your interests and passions, you may utilize a variety of platforms and channels, such as blogs, videos, social media, or online forums. You can also join a variety of communities and groups, like courses, clubs, or volunteer organizations.

Donate to the Community and Make a Trace

Retirement offers an opportunity to contribute to society and the world in ways that have a good and enduring influence on others, as well as to give back to your community and leave a legacy. You may express your ideas and views and give your retirement years more meaning and purpose by giving back to the community and leaving a legacy.

You may leave a legacy and give back to your community in several ways, including:

- Offering your time, abilities, and talents to a cause or organization that matters to you and could use your assistance—such as a hospital, school, or charity—is known as volunteering.

- Mentoring is the practice of imparting your knowledge, expertise, and insight to a student, colleague, friend, or anybody else who can learn from you and gain from your direction.

- Giving money, products, or other assets to a cause or organization that you favour and that may benefit from your resources, such as a foundation, museum, or church, is known as donating.

- Creating, which is the process of coming up with an original work of art, music, podcast, book, or other creative expression that may impact or inspire others.

- Teaching is the act of transferring your information, abilities, and experience to a class, group, or audience—someone who can use your education and benefit from your teachings.

You must do certain actions to contribute back to your community and leave a legacy, such as:

I. Identify your values and beliefs. List the things that are important to you and that influence your choices and behaviour, such as your ethics, morality, and principles.

II.   Identify your causes and organizations. List the causes and organizations that you wish to support or join, such as environmental, social, or cultural issues or organizations.

III.   List the methods and resources you may utilize, such as volunteering, mentoring, giving, producing, or teaching, to give back to your community and leave a legacy.

IV.   Make a good and long-lasting effect on others by giving back to your community and leaving a legacy, or by beginning and continuing to make contributions to society and the wider globe. Websites, applications, and podcasts are just a few of the tools and resources you may utilize to leave a legacy and give back to your community.

V. Share your accomplishments and effects with your loved ones, coworkers, and friends.

VI. Celebrate your accomplishments and impacts. You may highlight your successes and influences by using a variety of venues and channels, such as blogs, videos, social media, and online forums.

Conclusion

Now that you've finished the book, we hope you have a better understanding of how to organize, get ready for, and enjoy your retirement as a woman. Retirement is a gratifying and exciting journey with a plethora of chances and possibilities, but it's also a difficult and personal process that needs careful preparation and execution.

The following subjects have been discussed in this book:

> ➤ How to evaluate your existing circumstances and project your retirement income and costs

➤ How to prioritize your retirement requirements and desires and define your retirement vision and objectives

➤ How to increase your retirement account balance and choose the finest investments and retirement accounts

➤ How to guard your retirement savings and control the risks associated with longevity, inflation, and market volatility

➤ How to develop a withdrawal plan and diversify your sources of income

➤ How to budget for your requirements for insurance, long-term care, and medical care

➤ How to cope with the psychological and social changes that come with retirement

➤ How to continue your interests and passions after retirement

➤ How to leave a legacy and give back to your community

However, retirement planning is a continuous process that has to be reviewed and updated regularly rather than a one-time occurrence. Your retirement requirements, aspirations, and circumstances should all evolve as your life does. As a result, to keep your retirement plan current, practical, and efficient, you must regularly review it and make changes as needed.

The following are some actions you may take to routinely examine and improve your retirement plan:

❖ Examine your retirement plan annually, or more often if a significant event occurs in your life, such as a shift in your income, spending, health, family, or profession.

❖ Evaluate your priorities and retirement objectives to make sure they still reflect your beliefs, passions, and dreams.

- ❖ Check to determine whether your retirement income and spending are still realistic, adequate, and sustainable.

- ❖ Check if your retirement portfolio still represents the asset allocation and risk tolerance you have always wanted by rebalancing it.

- ❖ Review your retirement plan to make sure it still lowers your tax obligation and satisfies your requirements and goals for retirement.

Retirement planning is a psychological and emotional problem in addition to a financial one. Retirement has a lot of advantages and delights, but it also has a lot of risks and challenges. As a result, you must be aware of, ready for, and able to overcome the typical obstacles and traps of retirement with fortitude and hope.

Retirement presents several frequent hazards and obstacles, including:

- Having ambiguous or unreasonable expectations, which might cause regret, annoyance, or disappointment

- Having a variable or inadequate income, which might cause stress, worry, or other financial difficulties

- Receiving insufficient or expensive medical treatment, which might result in issues, difficulties, or emergencies

- Engaging in little or unfulfilling social contacts, which may result in sadness, loneliness, or isolation

- Lacking direction or significance, which may result in ennui, emptiness, or hopelessness

Among the methods and approaches you might use to get beyond the typical obstacles and difficulties of retirement are:

a. Be flexible and adaptive to the changes and uncertainties of retirement.

b. Establish clear and reasonable expectations.

c. Use a variety of tools and resources, as well as expert advice and support, to help you manage your retirement funds and taxes.

d. Take charge of your physical, mental, and emotional well-being and make use of numerous perks and programs to assist you in paying for your medical treatment and long-term care.

e. Keep up and grow your social network, and take part in different events and activities to keep yourself involved and linked to other people.

f. Discover and follow your interests and passions. - Make use of all available channels and chances to express and realize your potential.

Putting together a retirement plan is both a task and a success. A significant turning point that signifies the conclusion of your working years and the start of your golden years is retirement. As a result, you should recognize and celebrate your retirement milestones and accomplishments and give yourself a gift for your diligence and hard work.

Here are a few ideas for commemorating your retirement milestones and accomplishments:

- Host a retirement party or get-together with your loved ones, coworkers, and friends to discuss your goals, recollections, and retirement anecdotes.

- Take a retirement vacation or visit somewhere you've always wanted to see and explore the sights, sounds, and cultures of a different location.

- Purchase a retirement present for yourself or treat yourself to something you've always desired, then enjoy the joy and contentment that come with having it.

- Write a note to your former company, colleagues, or clients summarizing your retirement path, accomplishments, and expressions of thanks.

- Make a scrapbook for your retirement, or gather and arrange your retirement pictures, records, and artefacts, then present them imaginatively and poignantly.

We hope you have loved reading this book as much as we have liked creating it. This marks the conclusion of the book. We hope that this book has given you useful knowledge, ideas, and advice on how to organize, get ready for, and enjoy your retirement as a woman. We hope that this book has motivated you to act and realize your retirement goals.

We hope you will have a happy, healthy, and meaningful retirement life and wish you all the best of luck on your retirement journey.